The Life and Times of a

Drop of Water

Chicago, Illinois

Printed and bound in China
by WKT Co., Ltd

10 09 08
10 9 8 7 6 5 4 3 2

**Library of Congress Cataloging-in-
Publication Data**
Royston, Angela.
  The life and times of a drop of water : the water
cycle / Angela
Royston.
     p. cm. -- (Fusion)
  Includes bibliographical references.
  ISBN 1-4109-1925-0 (library binding-hardcover) --
ISBN 1-4109-1956-0
(pbk.)
ISBN 978-1-4109-1925-0 (Hc)
ISBN 978-1-4109-1956-4 (pbk.)
  1. Hydrologic cycle--Juvenile literature. I. Title. II.
Fusion
(Chicago,
Ill.)
  GB848.R69 2006
  551.48--dc22
                                    2005016489

Acknowledgments
The author and publishers are grateful to the
following for permission to reproduce copyright
material: Alamy (John Foxx) p. 18; Alamy/Shout
pp. 16–17; Corbis (Patrik Giardino pp. 8–9; Getty
Images/Stone pp. 15, 20–21, 23, 24–25; Robert
Harding Picture Library/JJ Travel Photography
pp. 10–11; Science Photo Library pp. 26–27 (G. Brad
Lewis), 6–7 (Michael Marten), 12–13 (Ted Kinsman);
Science Photo Library/Holt Studios International
(Nigel Cattlin) pp. 4–5.

Cover photograph of a drop of water, reproduced
with permission of Science Photo Library
(Oscar Burriel).

Illustrations by Darren Lingard.

The publishers would like to thank Nancy Harris
and Harold Pratt for their assistance in the
preparation of this book.

Every effort has been made to contact copyright
holders of any material reproduced in this book.
Any omissions will be rectified in subsequent
printings if notice is given to the publishers.

The paper used to print this book comes from
sustainable resources.

Disclaimer
All the Internet addresses (URLs) given in this book
were valid at the time of going to press. However,
due to the dynamic nature of the Internet, some
addresses may have changed, or sites may have
changed or ceased to exist since publication. While
the author and publishers regret any inconvenience
this may cause readers, no responsibility for any
such changes can be accepted by either the author
or the publishers.

Contents

Some words are printed in bold, **like this**. You can find out what they mean on page 30. You can also look in the box at the bottom of the page where they first appear.

Just a Drop of Water?

The photo shows one drop of water. It is a drop of clear liquid that you take for granted. You probably do not even notice it in your everyday life. Yet water has been around almost since Earth began. Without it, you would not exist.

A drop of water never stays the same for long. It is always changing. Sometimes it joins with other drops to form a big flow of water. Sometimes it is an invisible gas that floats in the air. At other times it is solid ice. Yet it is always water.

Water moves from the land and sea to the sky—and then back to Earth. This never-ending cycle is called the **water cycle**.

Would you like to see where this drop of water came from? What might happen to it? Read on and find out.

Three states

Water can exist in three states: solid ice, liquid water, and gas.

water cycle   movement of water from the sky—to the

▼ A drop of water is about to fall from a leaf.

Raindrops

Raindrops form in clouds in the sky. A cloud is made up of millions of tiny drops of water. The drops are liquid. They are so light they can float in the air. They are very tiny. A single hair on your head is ten times wider than one of these drops! Each drop is made of tiny water **molecules**. A molecule of water is the smallest part of water that exists.

We will follow one drop in the middle of a rain cloud. It is having a bumpy ride! It gets dragged up to the top of the cloud. Then, it tumbles down to the bottom. Other drops crash into it. They join together to make a bigger drop.

The drop is dragged up again to the top of the cloud. It gets bigger and heavier. It soon becomes too heavy to float. Then, as a raindrop, it falls down to Earth.

Cloud fact

Clouds look gray before a storm. As the drops of water join together, the cloud gets thicker. The cloud is too thick to let much light through, so it looks dark.

▼ Air and water drops move up, down, and around inside a thundercloud.

Disappearing Act

What a downpour! The raindrop lands in a puddle. More raindrops land on the ground. The puddle gets deeper.

The rain stops and the sun comes out. The sun warms up the tiny water **molecules**. Molecules are the smallest parts of the water. As the water gets warmer, its molecules get more **energy**. Energy is the ability to move. The molecules start to move faster and faster.

Soon, the molecules are moving very fast. Some of them leap from the puddle and drift into the air. The liquid water is changing into a gas called **water vapor**. When a liquid changes to a gas, it **evaporates**. Millions of other molecules evaporate into the air. The puddle slowly gets smaller. Soon, the puddle dries up.

Water fact

After a shower of rain on a hot day, you can sometimes see steam rising from the ground. This is the water evaporating, and then turning back into tiny drops.

A cyclist rides through ▶ a puddle of water.

Floating in Air

The drop of water is not a liquid anymore. It is a gas. Now, the water **molecules** are so spread out you cannot see them. The water molecules drift upward with the air. The air gets cooler as they drift higher. The molecules begin to cool down.

The cooler molecules have less **energy**. They slow down and move closer and closer together. They start to change from **water vapor** back into liquid water. When a gas changes to a liquid, it **condenses**. The molecules form a mist of tiny drops. Now, you can see them. They are part of a small cloud.

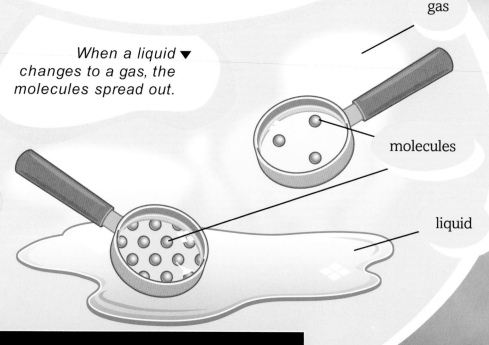

When a liquid ▼ changes to a gas, the molecules spread out.

gas

molecules

liquid

condense   turn from a gas into a liquid

A strong wind pushes the cloud over cities, farms, lakes, and canyons. The cloud gets bigger and thicker. The wind blows it toward a high mountain range. The water drops are pushed up into even colder air.

▼ *These clouds have blown for miles.*

Snowstorm

It is very cold over the mountains. The water drops **freeze**. They change from liquid into tiny pieces of solid ice. Now, the cloud is made of millions of tiny **crystals** of ice.

Several crystals stick together to form a beautiful pattern —a snowflake! Other snowflakes are also forming inside the cloud.

The snowflake whirls and tumbles around the cloud. More ice crystals stick to it. The snowflake grows bigger and bigger and heavier and heavier! It has become too heavy to stay afloat in the cloud. It drifts slowly down through the air. Where will it land?

Snow fact

Every snowflake has six sides. Yet no two snowflakes are exactly alike. The largest snowflake ever recorded was 15 inches (38 centimeters) wide! It fell in Montana in 1887.

crystal	solid with a symmetrical (regular) shape
freeze	change from a liquid into a solid
microscope	machine that makes things look bigger than they really are

▼ *This is a small part of a snowflake seen through a **microscope**.*

River Journey

The snowflake lands on top of a mountain. More snowflakes fall on top of it. It is freezing cold. You could not survive for long up there. Yet the snow will stay here all winter.

In spring, the air begins to warm up. The solid snow and ice start to **melt**. Each snowflake becomes a drop of liquid water again. The drops join together and trickle down the mountainside. The trickle joins up with other trickles of water. Soon, they become a mountain stream.

The stream tumbles over a waterfall. It crashes into a deep pool below. The mountain stream joins with other streams. It makes a river of rushing water. The water smashes into rocks and pushes fallen branches down the river.

Water fact

The world's longest river is the Nile River in Africa. It is 4160 miles (6695 kilometers) long!

melt   change from a solid into a liquid

▼ *A canoe hurtles down a waterfall.*

Flood water

The river has flowed away from the mountains. It is moving across flatter land. The river passes through fields, forests, and towns. Remember, it is spring. **Melted** snow fills the river with more water than usual. The people who live near the river are worried. The water level is rising!

River water can ▶ sometimes flood over roads and into houses.

The river becomes narrower as it flows through a town. The water piles up in front of a bridge. Then, it spills over the river bank. It floods into the town.

The river floods the streets. Some of the water creeps under a doorway into a kitchen. I hope this is not your house! The water stays here for a few days. Then, the flood level begins to drop. The water trickles out of the house. It flows down a drain in the road and back into the river.

Plants and animals

The river winds its way toward the sea. Some of the river water flows into a shallow pool. It flows near a herd of cows. One cow sticks out her long, slimy tongue. Slurp! She licks up some drops of water and swallows them.

The drops of water tumble through her four stomachs. The water moves into her intestines. It passes through the walls of her stomachs and intestines and into her blood. The cow's blood carries the water all around her body.

Some of the blood reaches a part of the cow's lungs. One drop of water leaves the cow's blood. It squeezes through the thin wall into her lungs. The water **evaporates** inside the cow's lungs. It changes from a liquid to a gas. It has become **water vapor**.

With one spluttering puff, the cow breathes out the water vapor. The tiny water **molecules** float into the air. They drift upward until they hit cold air again.

Did you know?

The human brain is 75 percent water! In fact, all living things are between 60 and 90 percent water.

Tap Water

The water **molecules** fall as rain again, this time into a lake. This lake provides water for villages, towns, and cities. It is called a **reservoir**. The water is pumped from the reservoir to a water-treatment center. Here, it is cleaned.

The clean water leaves the water-treatment center. It flows through pipes to a town. Some of the water flows into a tap in a kitchen. This is your home! You turn on the tap.

Cleaning water

*The water from a reservoir is pumped to the top of a water tower. Then, it is sent through underground pipes to a water-treatment center. There, the water trickles through thick layers of sand and gravel. This gets rid of the dirt. A chemical called chlorine is poured into the water. The chlorine kills the **germs**. Now, the water is clean enough to drink.*

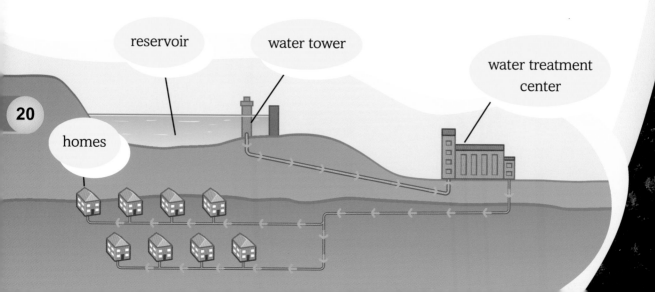

reservoir

water tower

water treatment center

homes

▼ A dam holds the water in this reservoir.

germs   tiny living things that can make you sick

reservoir lake that supplies water to villages, towns, and cities

Glug, swallow!

You feel thirsty. You pour yourself a drink of water. The water goes into your mouth. You swallow. The water is pushed down your throat into your stomach. You need to drink a lot of water every day. In fact, your body is about 60 percent water!

Most of the water squeezes through the walls of your stomach and intestines into your blood. Some of it stays in your body for several months. Yet some of it will not stay in your body for long.

Later, some of the water passes through your **kidneys**. Your kidneys produce a waste liquid called **urine**. The urine trickles down a narrow tube to be stored in your **bladder**. Your bladder becomes very full. You slam the bathroom door shut. Now, you empty your bladder.

Water fact

You cannot survive for more than a few days without drinking water. Your body would dry out, and you would die.

bladder	stretchy bag inside the body where urine is stored
kidney	body organ that filters waste chemicals and water from the blood to make urine
urine	mixture of water and waste chemicals from your body

In the U.S., a household uses about 98 gallons of water per day:

Water used for:		Amount of water used:	
Washing dishes		1 gal.	1%
Faucets		11 gal.	11%
Leaks and other uses		12 gal.	12%
Showers and baths		14 gal.	14%
Washing clothes		15 gal.	15%
Toilets		20 gal.	21%
Watering lawns and filling pools		25 gal.	26%

Down the drain

The liquid that leaves your body is yellow **urine**. It is a mixture of water and waste chemicals. The urine flows into the toilet. You flush the toilet. A gush of water swirls the urine down a pipe. Then, the water flows into a large underground pipe called a **sewer**.

The sewer joins up with a big tunnel. Dirty water from washing machines, showers, streets, and toilets flows through the tunnel. If you were down here, you would certainly have to hold your nose!

The dirty water flows into a sewage plant. Here, it trickles through beds of gravel, sand, and **charcoal**. These beds remove most of the dirt. Now, the water is clean enough to flow into a river and out to sea.

charcoal burned wood

◄ *This is a sewage plant. Dirty water flows through the beds. The beds remove dirt and clean the water.*

Germs are killed in this bed.

Solid waste is removed in this bed.

Drop in the Ocean

The river water mixes with the salty seawater. What will happen to the drop of water now? It might become part of a wave that crashes onto the coast. Or it could drift into the deeper ocean. It could sink below the surface and get swallowed by a fish.

What if the drop sinks deeper? Then, it will become part of the cold, dark water at the bottom of the ocean. It could stay there for centuries.

Yet perhaps the drop will rise back to the surface. The water will be warmer there. The drop might **evaporate** to become gas.

Then . . . well, the **water cycle** goes around forever. You had better leave the drop of water to run its cycle and get back to your own life!

Ocean fact

97 percent of the world's water is in the oceans.

The Water Cycle

Everything that happens to the drop of water in this book happens every day all around the world. Drops of water are forever changing—from gas to liquid, and from liquid to gas.

2

Clouds are blown through the air.

ocean

1

Water **evaporates** and becomes **water vapor**.

The **water cycle** is the movement ▶ of water from the land and sea to the sky—and then back to the land and sea.

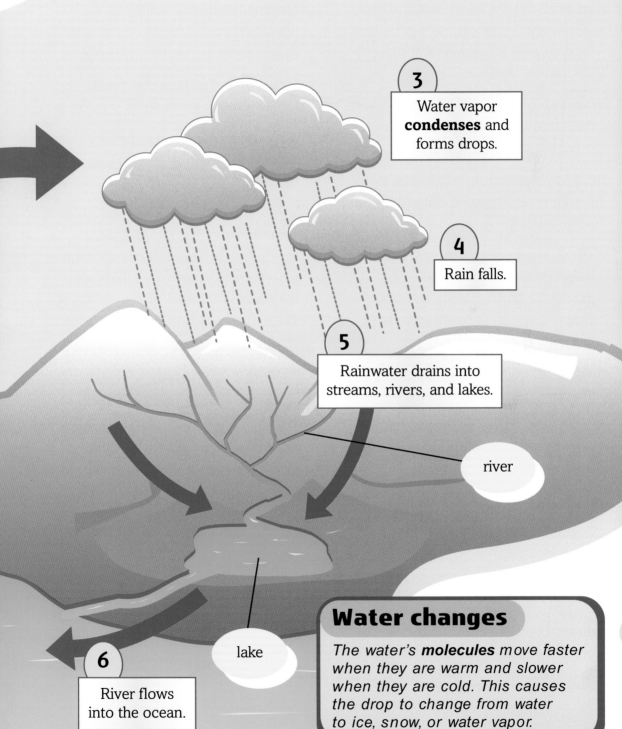

3 Water vapor **condenses** and forms drops.

4 Rain falls.

5 Rainwater drains into streams, rivers, and lakes.

river

lake

6 River flows into the ocean.

Water changes

*The water's **molecules** move faster when they are warm and slower when they are cold. This causes the drop to change from water to ice, snow, or water vapor.*

Glossary

bladder stretchy bag inside the body where urine is stored. When your bladder gets full, you feel the need to use the bathroom.

charcoal burned wood. As dirty water runs through charcoal, the charcoal traps the dirt.

condense turn from a gas into a liquid. As a gas cools, it condenses more quickly.

crystal solid with a symmetrical (regular) shape. All crystals of a particular substance are the same shape. They all fit together to make a regular pattern.

energy ability to move something or make something happen

evaporate change from a liquid into a gas. The warmer a liquid becomes, the faster it evaporates.

freeze change from a liquid into a solid. Water freezes into ice.

germs tiny living things that can make you sick. Many kinds of germs multiply fast in water.

kidney body organ that filters waste chemicals and water from the blood to make urine

melt change from a solid into a liquid. When ice melts, it changes to liquid water.

microscope machine that makes things look bigger than they really are

molecule smallest part of many substances, such as water. The molecules of any particular substance are all the same.

reservoir lake that supplies water to villages, towns, and cities. Some reservoirs are made by building a dam across the end of a river valley. Then, the river floods to form a lake.

sewer large pipe that collects waste water from streets and buildings. Sewers are usually underground.

urine mixture of water and waste chemicals from your body. About half the water you lose from your body every day is urine.

water cycle movement of water from the land and sea to the sky—and then back to the land and sea

water vapor water as a gas. Water vapor is invisible. Clouds and steam are water drops that have condensed from water vapor.

Want to Know More?

There is a lot more you can find out about the water cycle:

Books to read

- Ballard, Carol. *How We Use Water*. Chicago: Raintree, 2005.

- Harman, Rebecca. *The Water Cycle: Evaporation, Condensation, & Erosion*. Chicago: Heinemann Library, 2006.

- Parker, Steve. *The Science of Water: Projects and Experiments with Water Science and Power*. Chicago: Heinemann Library, 2005.

Websites

- http://ga.water.usgs.gov/edu/watercycle.html

  Check out this website to view a diagram of the water cycle and to follow a drop of water through the water cycle! Also, try visiting the activity center section. Sponsored by the U.S. Geological Survey.

- http://www.epa.gov/safewater/kids/index.html

  Visit this website to learn some interesting facts about water and to play some cool games! Sponsored by the U.S. Environmental Protection Agency.

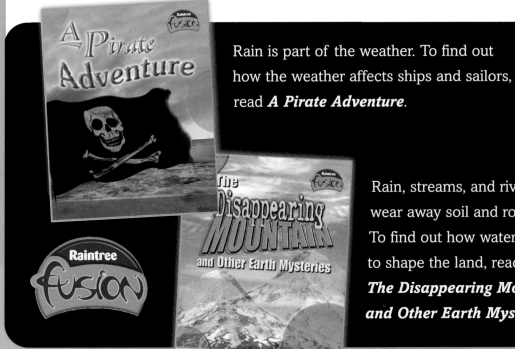

Rain is part of the weather. To find out how the weather affects ships and sailors, read **A Pirate Adventure**.

Rain, streams, and rivers wear away soil and rocks. To find out how water helps to shape the land, read **The Disappearing Mountain and Other Earth Mysteries**.

Index